The Phoenix Living Poets

NATURE WITH MAN

The Phoenix Living Poets

NATURE
WITH MAN

by
JON SILKIN

CHATTO AND WINDUS

THE HOGARTH PRESS

1965

Published by
Chatto and Windus Ltd
with The Hogarth Press Ltd
42 William IV Street
London WC2

★

Clarke, Irwin and Co Ltd
Toronto

Printed in Great Britain by
T. H. Brickell and Son Ltd
The Blackmore Press, Gillingham, Dorset

Contents

Acknowledgments

Acknowledgments are due to the following: *Agenda, Alarum, Avon Books* (N.Y.), *Birmingham Bulletin, Clare Market Review, Il Contemporaneo, Encounter, Flash Point* (E. J. Arnold), *Geste, Glasgow Herald, The Glasgow Review, Irish Times, Jazz Poems* (Studio Vista), *Marxist, New Durham, New Opinion, Neue Deutsche Hefte, Of Books and Humankind* (Routledge), *The Observer, P.E.N.* (1963), *Poetry and Audience, Poetry Review, The Review, Scope, Sewanee Review, Shenandoah, Stand, Time and Tide, The Times Literary Supplement, Universities' Poetry* (4 and 5).
Also to: *New Poetry B.B.C.* (Terence Tiller), *B.B.C. Scottish Television, Granada T.V., The Poets' Voice* (George Macbeth).
The first eight of the 'Flower' poems were broadcast in *The Living Poet* (George Macbeth); a smaller group appeared in *Granta* (then edited by John Barrell), and the first nine were published in pamphlet by Northern House (Leeds).

Nature with Man

The lank summer grass
As it is, bent and wailing;
A scorching wind
Scours a whole plain of it.
Dust still oppresses. Then
As if the earth received
A bruise a pool of brown
Slime erupts slowly
From among the stems. Summer mud . . .
Hot and stagnant. The grass stalks
Stand pricked without root
In the rimless mud . . . in what eye.
On some field of grey stone
A white sud of saliva,
So fine it seems a mildew,
Agonizes over the crop.

But are the humans here? Nature
Had a human head. The mouth
Turned on its long neck, biting through
Scale, sinew; and the blood
Carried through the flesh
Beyond the ends of veins
As the severed head
Rolled into the bullrushes.
This limp and useless
Going off among tall weeds
Has soured the earth, whose body
Decays and perishes.
As for the pain
That suds onto the stone;
That, simply, is pain.

9

How much else is there?
There is only one head.
But it has several minds
Which still give out
Great reticulations
Of ideas, nets wilful and sharp
Over it; binding it
In pride and thought that cut
The smiling face of pleasure.

'O pity, pity, pity'?
But the weedy soul is shrinking.
Nor can it see how
To join itself unto
The membered flesh. The whole
Of nature is turning slowly
Into an eye that searches
For its most developed
And treacherous creature, man.
Monstrous and huge eye:
The entire process
Of nature perverted
Into the search for him.

A Kind of Nature

To Leonard Clark. For Leslie Norris

Keats' vision of Langstone:
Land and sea separate,
The first, sorts of mist. Sea fumes
Through a ship in sails
Coming thinly on.
The land fumes; so it seems
It too sifts through the ship.
Men's made things, images of them,
Replace what we have learnt
Of trees that hold the soil,
Or flowers, seen closely.
Their beauty still remains.
Not nature's, but the eye's,
Whose ligaments and moisture
Contain flowers that were flowers
Seen often. Oils of seed
In liquid chain held in
The lemon's crystalled sharpness
And green pulps of simple cabbage.
Great England. O what laughter
Of water ripples into your vegetables,
Or slender sweetness through blades,
The delicate grasses of sensibility
Purple, pale violet, or lilac,
The three leafed clovers
Spread into curtseying
Demurely nubile.
Take care of Nature. Keats'
Vision must stay: a trope
For critics, merchandise
For types of shopkeeper

And poet; and be the sacredness
We use in churches
To justify 'the benign vision'
Of an indifferent God
Swollen with pulps of man.
He is our carnivore
And we, His feeling plants.
And that's the complex part.
For if He cared more
We might, like children
Put on trust, treat one
Another with more care.
For the price of having the Father
Would be obedience;
His images, our flesh.
But if we are alone
Like stones in a huge field
Stupidly brutal,
Where is the trust, that fine
Sharpness of moral care
Inhered in each recess
Of lemon consciousness?
Nothing will guide
The pressed stones open
To the waters of heaven
That erode us, as we nudge
Wear and crack each other;
Though we are a beauteous
Gift of each other.

Soon

Our boat gorged up
Between shores, whose vines
Held light, pushing it onto
The sea underneath.
Nothing spoke. The cut
Waters spent themselves
Inches between the craft
And close shore. Grapes tangled
With the mast, and fell.
Through a chasm of plants
We emerged, and there,
Wanted breath. Our sides,
And foreheads, creased wetly.
We lived, we knew. And then
Anchored into the space
We came on, without speech.
And of one movement
Went onto land. Through woods
Where dust with green
Spines of fir passed
By the shoe, we climbed.
We came to tilled fields
Whose corn had been grasped,
Or whose nuts, & vines,
Waited a man's hand.
But nowhere was that creature,
His mule not seen. Until
Over a plateau with
Some cypresses we saw
The temple. The queer thing
Between us was the silence
Thinning the air; its clearness
Bore the sun on us.

And here, like flies, we moved
Distractedly, with membranous
Hands raised upwards.
And each of us, I felt,
If he could have believed
Would have spoken; admitting
The cold nourishment of fear.
Fear we had not:
Save for our half-fear
Stronger than all. Tired
Of this I moved up to
A cypress, erect, tapering.
And picked up from the ground,
With fangs open, the ends
Shaped like small clubs,
A cone. I lifted it:
Emissions of seed spilled
Over my hand, infesting
It with seminal decay,
Leaving on the core inside
A speckled whiteness.

The Distraction

(For Ian Hamilton)

Yesterday
She gathered flowers into
Her arms; and though I cannot
Tell you what the life
Was named, I know that these
Were last flowers; some final
Intermission of colour
Before the season falls.
So that in this poise
In which a woman took
A mortal thing to her body
There seemed a poignancy;
As though the figure of
Proserpine near Dis
Breathed into that bent form:
One flower entering
Another at her breast.
And all the time she gathered
The fairest delicacy
The dead nourish in nature
Nor for man's delight but
For the whole exacting process
Of growth towards the earth.
Yet from the earth
Some pincering insect form
Emerged, as if it would
Draw them and death below;
As though the cold did not
Contract the spines of life
Closely enough to death.

The Religous West

You tell me the Christian religion must settle accounts. What accounts?
I see none. It has helped create a life fit even for pigs.

Priest in Old Play

One sees
But a heap of shoes
Beaten to trash.

Not one ritual's deterred.
Since 'pigs will always be pigs'[1]
And a knife help
As ever:—a pig for a pig.

'Light on a bare side,
A little tear of blood
And a cry: what could we want more?
If having these attributes
Of the martyr.
     I see one
Shoe of size, big as
A lap-dog, is moving
Out. Down with it.
See the sun, how it
Goes on illuminating
Its fragment central to it.
     He does live
Among us
Whose rigid desires made good
Aggravate all that
Perplexes man,
Fluttering within his flesh,
To unanimity
Through worship, action, attention to

The meticulous problems that taunt
The spirit. Borne against
The sun is some loose blood.
What's that? An ounce or so,
It would appal its kith
With its meagreness
As eggs their fly.
What's that, that is borne
Against the faultless sun?'

Slopt in wet, tugged loose,
It sprinkles through the seas
In tiny eggs of mud.

Slowly the sun,
Like half the face of God,
Seethes through the stained west –
Exultant, smeared, and tired
Of its labour, gorged on, and relished.[1]

[1]*Bialik, the Russian-Jewish poet*

Defence

(For Ann)

What 'one-in-five' can do
No man can quite do

She arrived late, with this motto:
'Time used in reconnaissance
Is not time lost'. Useful hint
On how efficient our defences
Would be. Sent from the *Home Office*
On 'Work of some importance'.
And 'The first thing' she said
'Is that there will be four minutes
Of preparation before
The thing is dropped. You should
Instruct persons to stand
In the centre of what room
They like – for the blast,
Unlike the bombs of the previous war,
Will draw the walls out.
There will be no crushing
Of flesh. Instead
On all sides walls will reveal
The citizen unharmed.' Here a question,
But 'No' she said 'we have
From our *Intelligence*
Absolute assurance
Our capital is not targeted.'
Total warfare, by arrangement.
And she was sure, when pressed.
'But there will be devastation
As we now suspect, in radius
Of forty four miles.
The water will be infected;

The light from the thing, astonishing;
Which though surprised by, we should
Not look at; but shelter
Behind some object "to reduce
Damage to the tissue"
From radiation; or shelter
Under brown paper;
Or, if you can, –
Sheets soaked in urine.'

So women who crotchet, stop that;
Men labouring whose issue is
The two-handed house, set that aside.
Girls big and delicate
With child, turn on your side;
You will melt. The ravelling spider
And the scorpion whose prongs itch
Will fuse in a viscoid
Tar, black as a huge fly.
The whole of nature
Is a preying upon.
Let man, whose mind is large,
Legislate for
All passionate things,
All sensate things: the sensuous
Grass, whose speech is all
In its sharp, bending blade.
Leave not a leaf, a stone
That rested on the dead
To its own dissolution.

She left then,
As if she were with her feet
Turning an enormous,
If man-made, pearl
As means of locomotion.

Community

You said, 'you make love to me
Like no other.' I did
Not ask if that implied
"Recently". For if
The dead are here, now discomforting us,
And though no one at all
May be so daft or childish
As to gaze at the wiped knives
And shuck the dead off, into after-life,
Yet there is our sex: and this,
With the abusing of it
Through urging it, and also
Threat of companions in
Our devouring, remains
A direction of bodily energies
I call "love". Such a word
Seems cynical: the contempt
Of the emancipated,
It hardens the mouth of every
Adolescent woman
Seeking marriage. I use it.
I saw: I felt then the flickering
Slender muscle strain
For completeness, and forcing back
The sheets, you under me
A determination of movement
With your vagina's lips
Taut as a bow – and the hill
Of living bone rush to me
As if the earth shifted.
There are no areas of
Our lives, isolated,
Life-giving, like benign

Liquid on the sand.
There is this: a creation
I am not yet ashamed
I helped to make. The dead, even,
Put to death by creatures
With a crude cleverness
More immune than instruments
That tease the genitals out,
Do not make this seem wrong.
We imitate, basely, but we imitate.
When I die I want
No ritual, only the strengthening
Of the passion to create love,
Not hindered by some mourning,
And perpetuated by
This simple image of
A pervasive hunger.

Processes

Not flesh; and spirit is
One part of this.

It is a softness not easily abraded;
Whose play, a slipping out of the summer's fingers
Detains me.

If it were
Your kiss fixed on my body
Not all of that
Would suffice.

Something that can be thought.
Though that smelted into
Mind's cold, yet
Upon the fingers.

Its pressures sink onto
The man inside the flesh
Who gropes after union.

So that the manifold thing
Is like the body which
Poor Plato whirled about in
Sick as war.

And you can feel that what
I'm speaking of is love.

I touch you; but mostly those
Charges your smile grows from

Until you are a gathering of forms:

The rose in mildews
Whose trenchant whorls
Of felt shape self-perfectingly
Cause to char inwards;

The idea itself, perishing
Against its will, like a man
Enlisted to fight
War's contradictions.

It is these things you seem like:
All of them:

Even the man.

The fatherless body melts
Of its enormous wounds.

Though if we'd bent over
This dying man, such care
Would be, like the adult's finger
Closed over by the child's hand,

A form of permanence.
But he has turned apart.

Evening

At the foot of the evening's marches
A clear water shifts,
The colour of an olive.

And reaches the short fire
Whose memory is a space.

I hear the crickets and frogs
Through smoke

Where grass shakes, delicately.

From the Italian of Ungaretti

Death Pain

To die
Like larks thirsting
In a mirage

Or like the quail
That has crossed the sea in
The first thicket
Because it has no
Wish
     any
More to fly

But not to
Live
On lament like
A blinded goldfinch

From the Italian of Ungaretti

Watch

A whole night
Thrown beside
A slaughtered friend with his mouth
Turned and grinning
To the full moon.
The congestion of his hands
Penetrating
My silence,
I write letters filled
With love.

I have never been
So fully
Attached to life.

From the Italian of Ungaretti

Rivers

This mutilated tree gives
Me support, left in this pot-hole.
It has the bitterness of a circus
Before or after the show.
I watch
The quiet passage of
Clouds over the moon.

This morning I stretched
Myself in an urn of water,
Like a relic, and rested.

The Isonzo scoured
Me like
One of its stones.

I pulled my four
Limbs together,
And went, like an acrobat,
Over the water.

Crouched by my clothes
Fouled with war, I inclined
My head, like a Bedouin,
To receive the sun.

This is the Isonzo.
And it is there I
Most see myself
In the universe
A compliant
Thread.

My pain is
When I do not believe
Myself in harmony.

But those hidden
Hands give as they knead me
A rare joy.

I have relived
The stages of my life.

The Serchio: from
Which have drawn, perhaps
For two thousand years
My country people, my father,
My mother.

This is the Nile
That has seen me be born,
And grow
And burn in ignorance on
Extending plains.

This is the Seine; and I mingled
In that muddiness learning each
Part of all myself.

These are my rivers confluent
In the Isonzo.

This is my nostalgia
That in each
One shines through me, now
It is night, and my life seems
A budding
Off of shades.

From the Italian of Ungaretti

No More Crying Out

Cease murdering the dead.
If you hope not to perish, if you
Want sound of them again,
Stop crying out, cease
The crying out of it.

They have a barely heard whispering,
No more than the increase of grass,
Happy where no man passes.

From the Italian of Ungaretti

The Child's Life

He lived, or started, to
Grow as a leaf. Thorns
That bud in mid-winter,
The jasmine whose pointed smell
Picks at the senses, and elicits
Secretions of eagerness
In the hanging basin of the loins,
In subdued weariness
Die off. Some different growth
Where assent is denied, where need
Admits and nourishes its creatures –
This growth became
His measure. Like a leaf,
He spread shade under him.
His humanness changed to
Plant vigour.
It seemed to him as if
Speech were constriction,
A crushing tight of silence;

cabbage —
moron

28

As though he could speak
But would not. As though
The human form and its
Consorting were a forgery
From Nature, poorly thieved.
We made him; and some of
Our anguish filled him, burst
Slowly from him, as the moisture of death
Intelligently released,
Moved away quietly.
A stiffening quietness
Showed through the face-skin, such as
We had not seen. He had
The impassivity
Of the veined leaf
To blown grit and smutched rain.
He grows with the soil.

[handwritten margin note:] not a child - but a replica - because it has not the quality of a child

Burying

It is not in the face.
That force has broken off
Which pressed through the ducts the liquids
Nourishing your life.

And absolutely as
You had not before been, with a
    Marked stiffening that

Composed your short frame,
The flesh settling noiselessly onto
    The compact bone.

A bricklayer tooled that space
You drew the entire process of your growth in
    And died in, gradually.

With no bodily pain,
But with grief, akin with the agèd; your face
    A mass of sea weed.

And after you had died,
Thickly pallid. I could not think
    There was no breath left.

I paid a few pounds for
Something to case your flesh, it seemed required
    By trade you should have.

Chewed pulp with fibre
Crushed into shape by the corrugation of men's will.
    A child would not have

Perceived the poorness in that.
You preferred nothing, with a likeness of absorbed
    Wills acting separately,

Such as the buriers have.

The psalm, as a shade
Of flower, touched merely
    Where you were.

I think that if I could
Have paid more for you,
There would have been more persons
Standing above that hole.
Much good might that do still
Although the mouth has gently
Chewed your flesh into
The ineradicable
Humus, the thriving muck
Which feeds the things we feed with;
For you were not honoured
Except with a thin box,
And the soil, which fastens
Each living thing to itself
Without ceremony or hate
Or anything casual

The Child

Something that can be heard
Is a grasping of soft fingers
Behind that door.
Oh come in, please come in
And be seated.

It was hard to be sure,
Because for some time a creature
Had bitten at the wood.
But this was something else; a pure noise
Humanly shaped

That gently insists on
Being present. I am sure you are.
Look: the pots over the fire
On a shelf, just put;
So, and no other way,

Are as you have seen them; and you,
Being visible, make them no different.
No man nor thing shall take
Your place from you; so little,
You would think, to ask for.

I have not denied; you know that.
Do you? Do you see
How you are guttered
At a breath, a flicker from me?
Burn more then.

Move this way with me,
Over the stone. Here are
Your father's utensils on
The kitchen wall; cling
As I lead you.

It seems you have come without speech,
And flesh. If it be love
That moves with smallness through
These rooms, speak to me,
As you move.

You have not come with
Me, but burn on the stone.

If I could pick you up
If I could lift you;
Can a thing be weightless?
I have seen, when I did lift you

How your flesh was casually
Pressed in. You have come
Without bone, or blood.
Is that to be preferred?
A flesh without

Sinew, a bone that has
No hardness, and will not snap.
Hair with no spring; without
Juices, touching, or speech.
What are you?

Or rather, show me, since
You cannot speak, that you are real;
A proper effusion of air,
Not that I doubt, blown by a breath
Into my child;

As if you might grow on that vapour
To thought, or natural movement
That expresses, 'I know where I am.'
Yet that you are here,
I feel.

Though you are different.
The brain being touched lightly,
It was gone. Yet since you live,
As if you were not born,
Strangeness of strangeness, speak.

Or rather, touch my breath
With your breath, steadily
And breathe yourself into me.

The soft huge pulsing comes
And passes through my flesh
Out of my hearing.

The Continuance

Your head had grown onto
Your knees; short arms were raised
With hands that pressed against
The temples. Each part formed,
It was fit to meet pressures on
The natural, linked flesh
Of yours inside hers.
The vessel's maternity stopped
Its involuntary, concerted
Nurture of your body.
You were expelled.
I think you did not weep;
You were red, smooth, raw,
Reliefed in your growth.

Something is asking to come from me
It is a mind that has no flesh.
Leave it. Leave it.
Something requires ease
But will not have the touch
Which first pervades the thought
Of one's own flesh, and is
Put then onto the child.
Something is weeping. It is no longer weeping.
It shall be left without
The hand which gives the flesh
Its nourishment. It feeds
Its cry with another cry; it weeps
Upon the bone, and sinks
Its separated pain
Into the bone, starting
A potent, tearless, grief
That had begun before.

Something has been Teased from Me

Something has been teased from me
Something insistent and tentative, as grass is
With soil; each binding, each nourishing, both.

We together were like them,
Knit, as the insistent roots of grass compact soil in a field:
A system of thread holding soil it eased into particles.

Their strength crumbles stone:
You allowed penetration. What can't be stopped must be
        nourished –
Pervading like grass, a sort of fire.

That would not quite do.
Grass does not feed itself, soil is bound by roots.
It is a composure the grass gives. You asked

For some change in me; insisted.
You shrilled, were acrid to the touch; but grass cannot
        change its roots.
It seeds itself in the soil, needing it; but is not soil.

My roots offended:
That tentative strength from which I pushed
Tall, seeded, sharp; whose webbed anchorage held you.

What could I have done?
I was loathed for what I was best, filled
You with liquids not yours. I seemed not good for you.

And slowly, I became
Undesired. What you needed,

You stopped me being:
A thing that cracked stone, ate it by means of roots.
I became reed delicate, a set of porous fibres.

It is not natural to
Grow by separation.

We did.
We pressed each other off, and grew through that.

The fruited thing persists.
It is corded, and thickly braided, like the unopened
        bluebell's flower.
It grows in you. It demands shape and blood
As it thickens to consciousness.

A single thickening sharpness lifts
Through moisture. It is nearly to be tolerated;
It has to be. A part of me fastens in you.

Grass sucks water and salts in,
As if it alone existed. This thing is more swollen.
But it is grass I think this bone and blood

Is like, persisting as grass, a blade of bone and flesh
Lifting to consciousness. It integrates
Into a flexible and feeling flesh.

As you lie down to
Give it its way, you turn on your side, lifting up
Your right thigh, shaped like dropping moisture, to your
        breast.

37

It demands strength
From you. Heaves. You heave. It is coming away.
It is good; it is to be endured.

It has to be. It comes away,
And as it does, is given breath.
Milk trickles through the tubules.
It lies beside you, put there. It will cry out.

And be nourished by you.
And grow like grass, wastefully. For now,
You hold it in your arms, and nurture it.

Dandelion

Slugs nestle where the stem
Broken, bleeds milk.
The flower is eyeless: the sight is compelled
By small, coarse, sharp petals,   — machine like
Like metal shreds. Formed,
They puncture, irregularly perforate
Their yellow, brutal glare.
And certainly want to
Devour the earth. With an ample movement
They are a foot high, as you look.
And coming back, they take hold
On pert domestic strains.
Others' lives are theirs. Between them
And domesticity,
Grass. They infest its weak land;
Fatten, hide slugs, infestate.
They look like plates; more closely
Like the first tryings, the machines, of nature
Riveted into her, successful.

38

A Bluebell

Most of them in the first tryings
Of nature, hang at angles,
Like lamps. These though
Look round, like young birds,
Poised on their stems. Closer,
In all their sweetness, malevolent. For there is
In the closed, blue flower, gas-coloured,
A seed-like dark green eye.
Carroway, grained, supple,
And watching; it is always there,
Fibrous, alerted,
Coarse grained enough to print
Out all your false delight
In 'sweet nature'. This is struggle.
The beetle exudes rot: the bee
Grapples the reluctant nectar
Coy, suppurating, and unresigned.
Buds print the human passion
Pure now not still immersed
In fighting wire worms.

Lilies of the Valley

Minute flowers harden. Depend
From thin bowing stem;
Are white as babies' teeth.
With broad leaves, immobile;
Are sheath-like, and fat.
What have these to do with beauty?
They must take you with
A fingering odour, clutches the senses,
Fills the creases and tightens the wind's seams,
As noise does. The plant is equipped.
Even then you don't like it.
Gradually though
Its predatory scent
Betters you, forces you, and more than
The protected rose creating
A sculptured distant adulation
For itself. This insinuates, then grapples you,
Being hungry; not poised, not gerundive.
Hard, and uncrushed, these flowerheads;
Like beads, in your palm.
You cannot destroy that conquering amorousness
Drenches the glands, and starts
The belled memory. Glows there, with odour.
Memorable as the skin
Of a fierce animal.

Peonies

It has a group of flowers.
Its buds shut, they exude
A moisture, a gum, expressed
From the sepals' metallic pressures.
Its colour shows between shields,
Cramped where the long neck
Swells into the head. Then they open.
They do it gradually,
Stammer at first. It is a confidence
Permits this; push aside
The shield, spray outwards,
Mount in height and colour
Upon the stem.
They claim the attention up there,
The focus of all else. Not aloof at all;
Brilliantly intimate,
They make the whites of others
A shrunk milk. They must draw
To them, the male ardours,
Enthusiasms; are predatory
In seeking them. Obliterate the garden
In flickerless ease, gouging out
The reluctant desires. Theirs is one rule,
And is found everywhere
Feeling transpires – extends
Its tendrils, helplessly grappling for
Passion of a different order
Than the peonies'.
What will be looked at,
However fleshily adequate,
Conquers the amorous.

By nature, a devourer. Cannot give.
Gives nothing.
In winter shrinks to a few sticks,
Its reversion, bunches of hollowness.
Pithless. Insensate, as before.

The Strawberry Plant

The rootless strawberry plant
Moves across the soil. It hops
Six inches. Has no single location,
Or root.
You cannot point to its origin,
Or parent. It shoots out
A pipe, and one more plant
Consolidates its ground.
It puts out crude petals, loosely met.
As if the business of flowering
Were to be got over. Their period is brief.
Even then, the fruit is green,
Swart, hairy. Its petals invite tearing
And are gone quickly,
As if they had been. The fruit swells,
Reddens, becomes succulent.
Propagation through the devouring
Appetite of another.
Is sweet, seeded, untruculent;
Slugs like it, all over.
It is nubile to the lips,
And survives even them. And teeth,
Insane with edible fury,
Of the loving kind.

A Daisy

Look unoriginal
Being numerous. They ask for attention
With that gradated yellow swelling
Of oily stamens. Petals focus them:
The eye-lashes grow wide.
Why should not one bring these to a funeral?
And at night, like children,
Without anxiety, their consciousness
Shut with white petals.

Blithe, individual.

The unwearying, small sunflower
Fills the grass
With versions of one eye.
A strength in the full look
Candid, solid, glad.
Domestic as milk.

In multitudes, wait,
Each, to be looked at, spoken to.
They do not wither;
Their going, a pressure
Of elate sympathy
Released from you.
Rich up to the last interval
With minute tubes of oil, pollen;
Utterly without scent, for the eye,
For the eye, simply. For the mind
And its invisible organ,
That feeling thing.

The Violet

The lobed petals receive
Each other's nestling shape.

We share the sun's benificence:
Frost, men, snowdrops.
Then the violet unfolds. Not an uncasing
Of the corolla, each petal compliant
To the purpose of survival, obedient to that; but as it feels
The sun's heat, that puberty
Pushes out from its earlier self-clasping
Two distinct, clenched halves. Stiffens then.
These fluttering portions that made
The bud, separately elect
To be the flower; the violet
Halves itself, pushing apart
In two separate forces;
It divides up itself, it becomes two violet portions.
It is not a conformation of members,
Each petal a tooth, an eyelash.
On the other hand, the violet is torn apart.
Its increase is by dividing;
Its stiffened petals push further apart.
It adheres to its nature; it has no maturity,
Other than this.
It requires courage, and finds that
In this unclasping of its self-worship: two palms tentatively
Open. Going both ways,
They absorb a huge circle
Of violeted air, an intent
Movement of embrace;
Created, exposed, powerful.
The air is coloured somewhat violet.
It costs itself much.

Milkmaids
(*Lady's Smock*)

Ridging the stalk's length,
The pith ducts. You'd think
The leaves found by water. Their openness
Guards them; a giddy, a careless
Effusion of stem. That is strength.
From the topmost, a flower triumphs.
From each undomestic
Flare, four petals; thrown wide; a flexible
Unplanned exuberance.
A veined fat is under
The svelte integument;
A kind of vegetative warmth.
From the centre, axial, determined
Extend the stamens, long by usage
For survival, and grouped
Round the curt stigma. Nothing less enslaved,
Less domestic to man, they are twice free.
Will wander through your plot in whole families.
You will not cut milkmaids down.

That tender, that wild, strength
Sucks the untrammelled consciousness up.
They mount the incline breathless
Pale violet. Their eyes wide,
They halt at the wire. This is the camp.
In silent shock a multitude of violet faces
Their aghast petals stiff, at the putresence
Of the crowd wired up. This halts them:
The showing bone; the ridges of famine,
Protrusions, want, reduction.
Silent also, they confront with their modesty
Of demeanour – the stiff fatigue
Of the sack jackets something altogether different

From those who supervise
In their soft, rigid cloth –
The prisoners confront
The unservanted faces of the plants.

Between their silences, comprehension; like the wire
Halted, staked, live.
Crowding through the tented cloth
That locust death, to each person.
For the flowers, the forked,
Upright sense of human
Creatures wanting patience, pulped, compounded into their
children.

Moss

'Patents' will burn it out; it would lie there
Turning white. It shelters on the soil; quilts it.
So persons lie over it; but look closely:
The thick, short green threads quiver like an animal
As a fungoid quivers between that and vegetable:
A mushroom's flesh with the texture and consistency of a
    kidney.

Moss is soft as a pouch.
There are too many shoots though, boxed compacted,
Yet nestling together,
Softly luminous.
They squirm minutely. The less compact kind
Has struggling white flowers; closed,
Like a minute bell's clapper;
So minute that opened then, its stretch seems wide.
The first grows in damper places.
With what does it propagate?
Quiet, of course, it adheres to
The cracks of waste-pipes, velvets,
Velours them; an enriching
Unnatural ruff swathing the urban 'manifestation':
The urban nature is basemented, semi-dark;
It musts, it is alone.

Here moss cools; it has no children;
It amplifies itself.
Could that over-knit fiction of stubbed threads reproduce
Defined creatures?
It hovers tentatively between one life and another,
Being the closed-road of plants,
Its mule; spreads only its kind –
A soft stone. It is not mad.

Reared on the creeping dankness of earth
It overspreads, smears, begrudges something
Though it is passive; spreads wildly.
It is immune to nothing;
You cannot speak of misery to it.

White Geranium

An astringent sweetness from
The veined leaves and round stem
Scrapes inside the nostrils.
Each part is haired,
Standing against dust. The Geranium
Shakes stiffly in the moving air.
Its stem, that has thin brown skin,
Extends a straight green shoot,
Unjointed, with five buds
The size of swollen pips.
It is the leaves' odour
Picks at the sinuses.
I want the buds to bear more than this.
Each small, tight thing is
Too formed to change much.
The haired surface protects
The thickening stem, which hardens
On its replenishing sap;
The leaves' smell
Is nearly incontinent.
The plants suffer themselves to be potted,
Warmed, conserved. They will
Shed whole branches;
Their size and quantity
Less than a shrub's.

Crowfoot (in water)

It is found, rooted,
In still water. A leaf,
Shaped like a kidney, floats
Leafing the underside of air, over water,
Taking in both, each side.
Inside the water
Are filaments of flesh-thread
Hair-drifting.
The flowers are white,
Simple, articulate.
Nothing smutches them.
Mouths of cattle, large
As sycamore trees,
Eat and compact stalk,
Leaf, stigma, and pigment
Into their food.

Shapes that no flower bred,
Not like any contour of nature,
Are piece-mealed
To a sponge of surging parts.

Articulate plant-speech does smutch
The ridged palate, bellying towards
The organ of hunger, minutely impotent.
The chopped articulation in the throat, –
Cattle's throat, – the woe
Is devoured. Crowfeet concerts
Its parts in a webbed cry.

If ripe, the seeds rear in
Dung casually dropped.

The rest persists under
The pond's rim. Can be devoured
To an inch of its life.

Small Celandine

Its petals close onto
A bland, contiguous sleep.
When open, they shoot from
That part large with organs,
Hips and face merged
In a thick, capable frame.
Its high crutched head is genitalled
For survival by display.
Flowers' conduct is supreme:
Fruit cankers, but petals age.
Insect life feeds on
Not it but its ripe seed,
Excreting over it; shard, rind, and succulence
Pinched by the sharp, smooth jaws.
A flower survives this. Small Celandine
Has sharp petals, its intensifying
Of their length, a self-absorption
That desires no further object.
Its lithe, green underside
Governs, with its greater thickness,
Each petal's direction. Leaves swaddle
The stem, as if near water.
It is indifferent to light, persisting with
Little sleep. It will
Not open or shut with what
Strikes into its senses.
It is insomniac
To that, merging it
With its form that presses little
Of itself on our minds.
We are not its leaf, its breathing.

Its adult, consciousless
Roots concert the sensuous
Nourishment of earth.

Goat's Beard and Daisy

They are closed, by noon,
Their petals held upwards.
In this sense, sleep is tension,
The closed tips of petals strained
Together, carefully.
If fertilized, they close earlier;
Conception achieved through
The stealth of a third. A plunderer
Covers the rooted creature's face.
The flower's silence is
Taken for deafness. As the insect hovers
Its passage is tautened through
Two kinds of organs' needs.
And what they have to give
Is as the bee nectars. Then they close.

The daisy has its mode.
It will close at night,
Or when rain gusts;
The soft, pouting stigma takes
The pungent, oily stamen's yielded pollen;
Grain is crammed in the gently
Insistent opening.
What the flower does it may do alone.
It will be beaten down, rather than open.
Rain squalls,
And sheets the swelling ground;
The closed daisy is fertilized.
When light comes, it responds,
Watching with one eye
A tree's bough
Wet all over, the antlered form
Stiff through girth, not pride.

Iris

Three extended tongue-like
Petals fall outwards.
A black, finely haired purple
Covers their extremities.
This colour suggests sap,
Like blood, gathering in pressure and staleness
At petal-ends that hang
Unable to sustain
Their weight. Where the joins
Of those three start
Are three smaller shapes,
Not striped like the first three.
Above these a further three,
As if a mimic of the second,
Suggesting consciousness.
A ridge is on each outer petal.
It is a fur of stigmas
Curved over the widening tongue,
Between three uplifted pale violet portions,
A coarse furred ridge, and like
One furred lip of the vulva.
In the curves of the flower
That are like an ear
One smaller ear listening advisedly at the larger,
Is the stamen, erect and white,
With its anther white. It is the male part
That is hidden, the female proffered.
Its colouring is determined,
Powerful; one band of it
Repeated, enforcing itself.
The species is prized for its shape,

Its chosen periodicity
Of flowering, a man's mind
Propped by growth that does
Not choose to grow.

Harebell

It is not bred by nature
To produce a succulence
With a seed nestling in that.
It is related by name to the Bluebell,
Which has flowers clinging
Like a braid round its fat stem.
The harebell is one flower,
Its solitariness
Bespoke by its colour, not blue
Nor violet; hovering between, precisely.
It is a spare delicate bell.
Inside it are three pale sugary stigmas welded
To each other at equal angles,
Not seen until looked for.
Its stem is thin as wire.
The flower looks down, and if
Lifted, looks fixedly
At the admirer.
Its silence halted between primness and beauty,
Its shape is wrung from the sounds of life round it
As a bell's sound forms the bell's shape from silence,
And resumes its demure integrity;
More precise, more shaped, than the bluebell;
More venturesome. More stirred, ungarrulous.
Stern as a pin.

Note on 'Flower' Poems

These poems have flowers as their 'subjects' but they can only loosely be called 'flower poems'.

The method is to take one particular species of flower, and to look at the flower quite closely. I also try to characterize the life and process of the flower and, in making all three substantial, to suggest certain correspondances with human types and situations. Yet although the poems are not only, and not simply, about flowers, they are not only or simply about human beings and their predicaments. They hover tentatively between the two, although whatever object or situation they temporarily absent themselves to they never lose sight of the flower. I am trying to find some common denominator that will pull together these two kinds of life. Even so, the poems do not poise themselves centrally between the two. They concentrate closely on the flowers, and it is towards their centrality they tend to draw *human* life as, in *The Peaceable Kingdom*, I was trying to draw human life in the direction of certain animals, and a peaceful consortium of all animals.

The poems work by describing the flowers but also move through them, re-creating some of our own feelings and attitudes, and where these differ from the flowers', suggesting sometimes possible changes in them.

Nearly all the flowers of these poems are wild, undomestic. The cultivated flowers are subject to the care of our hands, grown for our pleasure; cut down or rooted up if they're weeds. But if they are weeds, and are also insignificant, they may be allowed room. Such an action would flatter a man's vanity; it would permit him to praise his own compassion; his moral sensibility would be self-congratulated. We don't use the word 'pride' today, but that obstacle to honesty still stands.

These plants were all observed in the garden, the small hinterland where domestic and undomestic plants sometimes co-exist and sometimes compete. I see the garden, in fact, as a kind of human bestiary, containing in the several plants earlier developed and anticipatory examples of human types and situations. The first poem – *Dandelion*, for example – sees its subject as a seizer of space, and asks for political parallels to be made.

Moreover *Dandelion* and *A Bluebell* describe the flowers partly in terms of machines, machine shapes, or made objects and substances. The second poem (and I would pair these two) brings in explicitly what was implicit in the first: the theme of nature being a 'preying upon'.

The third and fourth poems are female in their analogizing (I'm of course only speaking of flowers). *Lilies-of-the-valley* – the flowers are seen as predatory, not beautiful. Their scent forces itself upon us with a meanness, and with something near to vulgarity. We succumb, and they conquer through being predatory.

The Peony might seem to be the same kind of flower as the Lily-of-the-valley, but it does not triumph through its odour; rather, it traps our sight. And whereas the Lily-of-the-valley means business, the aim of the Peony is to subjugate and enslave the admirer, and devour not only his attention but that of the whole bestiary.

The Strawberry Plant is in some ways a poem different from all the others. We cultivate the strawberries in order to devour them not look at them. This controlling fact places these creatures in a different relationship with the humans. The human appetite is roused; and that's an altogether different thing from looking at flowers even when the looking may lead to abuse – cutting them down for our rooms, or perceiving them as useful illustrators of 'human character'.

The next three poems are about benign flowers. The *Daisy* is closest to my conception of innocence, that is, an awareness, a complexion, got through experience (the opposite, therefore, of naivety) and where experience stands, largely, for vicissitude. It's the uncompromising simplicity of the Daisy's appearance that I'm trying to re-create; and it's the uncompromising quality that makes it so rich in this simplicity.

It is this uncompromising power that relates the *Daisy* to *The Violet*, a flower that for me presents one of the most complex of natures. The Violet is seen at first in its chrysalid stage, folded and self-absorbed. It's the tenacity of this self-absorption that individuates the flower. So that opened, it's this tenacity that carries through and dominates still. Its petals do not form a corolla subservient to the whole flower, whose purpose is survival. But in as much as the petals were, before, self-absorbed, they now spring apart and go opposite ways. *They change only to invert their original process.* The tenacity, the lack of uniform performance of the petals, which are the whole flower, visually speaking, characterize the Violet; just as what characterizes the activity of any person who makes something – an object, or a child – is the tenacity and the variety, not the consistency of the total activity.

Moss is a poem concerned with urban creatures whose sensuous shrinkage affects their capacity to propagate. Like the mule's, the organ is a shrunk thing incapable of increase. What is important here is that the stuntedness and sensuous dimunition is caused by the cramped, basemented environment. I am trying to characterize the stunted quality of these creatures, a quality that becomes eventually a barrenness.

Milkmaids differs from the other 'flower poems' in that it contains a direct confrontation between plant and human, instead of the implied partial analogy between the two creatures. The poem, I hope, avoids any tendency to anthropomorphize the flower; it tends to assert that the plant and the human are two separate but confronting parts of one society. The confrontation joins the creatures – what joins them even more is the total distress of the one and the capacity of the other to absorb this distress. The exchange is made more thoroughly because of the brutalized condition of the inmates of the camp; it is their degradation, but their will to persist also, that makes it possible for them to share their own and others' experience. It is this brutalized state that permits them to deeply perceive the openness of the Milkmaids, and, for the flowers' part, to absorb the condition of the humans emptied of 'the capacity to be patient under suffering'. Nor is there any reason for them to be patient. The Milkmaids absorb the experience of the human beings and are changed – one creature's mind changed by the condition of another, so deeply, that this change is inherited by their children.

One last point. To remove nature, to isolate it from human nature and then write about it, is an extremity as unproductive as the one which sees all nature as a (symbolic) version of man. Man is a part of Nature and to isolate one from the other, or to slide the one over the other, is to miss either the (related) complexity of both or the 'solidity' of each. The two are contiguous; and that is what I'm trying to get at in the 'flower' poems. If seen as contiguous, they can be seen as two components of a whole capable of mutual enrichment.

I ought to repeat that the majority of these poems are about *wild* flowers. The state, or monopoly capitalism controlling the individual's environment, this, I suppose, would make the (apparent) choice of the *wild* flower seem an acceptable symbol to some – if that were my meaning. But I don't see it like this – the wild flower as a lonely, isolated creature (there are, in any case, too many of them) standing for the isolated individual. There are these overtones, but I am not trying to anthropomorphize the flower. The wild flowers have a strength and tenacity that sometimes contrasts with the domestic plants; I am concerned with the former's vigorous contribution to the domestic land, their proximity to, not their symbolizing of, human beings and their activity. (*Nature with Man* would be an example of this; man grows from Nature and remains a part of it yet by virtue of his intelligence grows apart from it.) The injunctions of the state are an obvious enough possible danger to the individual, and society as a whole, but, of course, it depends on the state. Much social conformity results from the inability to resist and to change attitudes that have never been formulated by law. Some state practice, or sanction, like that of Nazi Germany, seems to have resulted from a political ordering that exacerbated certain forces it either permitted or deliberately brought into prominence. Not everything with a natural root has to be encouraged. I suppose I should add that I anticipate a time when the state will wither away. In the meantime I'm continuing to write about, among other creatures, wild flowers.